Young Man
WE GOTTA MAKE IT TO HEAVEN

Charleston, SC
www.PalmettoPublishing.com

Young Man, We Gotta Make It To Heaven
Copyright © 2022 by Decius Brown

First Edition

Hardcover ISBN: 979-8-88590-772-9
Paperback ISBN: 979-8-88590-773-6
eBook ISBN: 979-8-88590-774-3

Author photo courtesy of Dietrich Sharif Brown

Young Man WE GOTTA MAKE IT TO HEAVEN

DECIUS BROWN

For my son, Jonathan—
may you always walk in the ways
of the Lord.

Table of contents

Chapter 1   1
You Shall Live and Not Die

Chapter 2   9
Happy Birthday

Chapter 3   17
Live with Integrity

Chapter 4   27
Because I Said So

Chapter 5   37
The Mirror That Does Not Lie

Chapter 6   49
Say What?

Chapter 7   61
The Importance of a Team

Chapter 8   73
Flee from It

Chapter 9   85
Even in Your Dreams

Chapter 10   93
See It, and Hit It

Acknowledgments   99

Author's Note

Young man, this book was written with you in mind. My prayer is that it will encourage you to choose Christ each day, even though the world entices you to choose yourself and your own desires. I accepted Christ at a young age, and my journey as a young Christian was bumpy. It wasn't bumpy because following Christ was difficult; it was bumpy because I did not make my walk with Christ a priority.

I have failed God many times on my journey to Heaven. I now realize, however, that my failures did not define me and that obedience to God through Christ is what leads to my eternal reward. The time is now, young man, to stand up and take hold of that which is being offered to you—abundant life, even now, and eternal life through Jesus Christ. Let's take this journey to Heaven together. For nothing is worth comparing to the greatness that will be revealed.

Preface

I am blessed to be alive and to never have endured prison, considering my experiences with drugs, sex, violence, and other forms of ungodly behavior. I understand that my choices would have ultimately led to my destruction, and without an intervention from God, I was headed to Hell. I have failed God many times, and most of those failures were the result of my willingness to sin. My desire to please my flesh, my desire to fit in, and my desire to be what I thought a young man was supposed to be outweighed Christ's desire for my life. This book is for the young man who may be struggling to put Christ first, just as I struggled early on in my walk with Christ. It's for the young man who doesn't understand the process of putting Christ first. It's for the young man who needs to be encouraged to keep Christ first. It's for the young man who feels weighed down by worldly influences. This book is for anyone who wants to make it to Heaven—especially you, young man.

If you are reading this right now, you have the opportunity to receive the greatest reward that has ever been and will ever be offered. That reward is eternal life through Jesus Christ, spent in a place that Christians refer to as Heaven. Whether you have already accepted Jesus as your Savior or not, there is something you must know: it doesn't matter what you have done, where you have been, what you have been through, or what you are going through presently—Heaven is within your reach.

Jesus loves you unconditionally. He looks past all of your faults, bad habits, addictions, ungodly desires, doubts, and weaknesses because He desires that you live with Him for eternity. We are often tricked into believing that we are too messed up to receive God's love. The truth, though, is that God's love is not contingent upon our actions, our thoughts, our pasts, or our individual lives. Our great God loves us regardless of our faults, our failures, and even our successes. He loves us and wants to be with us so much that no matter how badly we have messed up, He only asks that we accept His Son, Jesus, as our Savior—the path to this reward He has prepared for us.

Imagine perfection in all that exists. A new Heaven, a new earth, a place where God Himself will be with us as our God, and we will be His people. Death will be no more; neither will there be mourning, crying, nor pain. All things will be made new (Revelation 21:1-5). That, young man, is where we are being called to live a life with our Creator for eternity. Yes, you are being called to a way of life that is different from everything you have seen and heard in this world. You, brother, are called to a life of separation from the rest of the world. You are called to a position of royalty! Jesus is the path that leads you to your great calling. This path that must be traveled by each of us is straight and narrow (Matthew 7:14). There are many temptations and worldly influences that lurk on the path's borders, hoping to entice travelers, like you, off the trail back into the carnal world. Negative influencers will lie to you, coercing you to believe that other trails, popular and conveniently roomy, are also a part of the narrow path God has chosen you to follow. No matter what, you must remember that your path will only have a few who have chosen to travel it. These few are the ones who are serious about strengthening their relationship with Christ. These few are the ones who will make it to Heaven.

Walking this path requires a very intentional approach, thus my reason for writing to you. I was once young, and my experiences with the world and with Jesus have taught me how to better walk the path that leads to eternal life. I accepted Christ at a young age. Being young, I often walked the path that was convenient for me. There were seasons when I tried very hard to walk in God's will, but honestly, more often I walked the much wider and most traveled path that was comfortable to me. As I grew older, instead of growing closer to Christ, I made my path wider and wider, camouflaging myself with the ways of the world. I still professed to be a follower of Christ (saved), but my actions said otherwise. Sure, I could have convinced anyone in any church that I was living the life of a Christian because I knew what was expected of me, but outside of church, I was a regular old sinner.

You see, while in church, it was easy to fit in. It was easy to do the things I was taught to do and the things I observed others doing all of my life. Clapping my hands, singing, and saying "Thank you, Jesus" was common and routine in church. I had already accepted Christ, and again, I knew what was expected of me, so the "saved" me was easy to display, even as I grew older and further away from Christ. Anyone who witnessed me in church, and not in the world, would have been convinced that my only gang was my church family and that Christ was who I was representing. They wouldn't have known about the rap music I was blasting on the way to church, turning the volume down just before I pulled into the church grounds. They also wouldn't have known about the worldly things I was involved in while in my community. If anyone witnessed me during my leisure time in my neighborhood, I'm sure they would not have linked me to the body of Christ because I was not representing Him.

Let's put this into perspective. Just as gangs are recognized by the color of their bandannas, tattoos, gang signs, and language, a follower of Jesus Christ is recognized by modeling for others the attributes of Jesus. A true follower of Christ exhibits godly character everywhere he goes, no matter who is around. A follower of Christ does not care about fitting into any other subgroups outside of those associated with Christ. We should stand out, we should be different, we should inspire others to inquire about Jesus because of our lifestyles (Matthew 5:14–16).

With full transparency, this book displays my understanding of the struggles that come with following Christ as a man, especially at a young age. However, with knowledge of who Jesus is and as a recipient of God's love, grace, mercy, and patience, this book was written to express the urgency of living a life worthy of the call. For you have been called by God (Ephesians 4:1).

Young man, I want you to make it. Let me help guide you on this path that leads to Heaven. First, may I offer you Christ?

Chapter 1

YOU SHALL LIVE AND NOT DIE

There is no therapy for feeling unloved. Only a realization of Jesus's love can remedy this hopeless feeling. The only rescue from the pit of feeling worthless is true recognition of the cross on which a ransom for you (and me) was paid (1 Timothy 2:6). This ransom's price we could never repay, and we will never be asked to try, but each of us will forever be indebted to Jesus for the great sacrifice He made for us: He gave His life! Still, all He asks of each of us is to believe in Him as our Lord and Savior and allow Him to live through us.

I thought I would surely die, but instead I woke up for school with a deathly stomachache; I was in so much distress that I vowed to never try it again. When you distance yourself from God, even for a moment, Satan has a way of making you feel that your life has no real value, no purpose. He helps you create this sad story about how people will miss you when you're gone and how they will wish they had loved you more or treated you better. He convinces you to think that once you're gone, all of your problems will go away, and things will be better. Convinced of these lies, I grabbed a bottle of pills, poured some into my hand, and with a glass of water swallowed what I thought was more than enough to release me from this life. Satisfied that my troubles would be over soon, I looked around my room for the last time, lay on the bottom bunk bed, thought about my family and friends, and went to sleep. I was in the seventh grade.

The next morning, I slowly opened my eyes. Immediately aware of my surroundings, I was surprised yet unexpectedly relieved that I had survived the night. The feeling in my stomach, however, was an excruciatingly painful reminder of my foolish attempt to end what did not belong to me—my life.

Many would debate whether I would have opened my eyes in Hell if my suicide attempt had been successful. However, this debate is not my present concern. My goal is to shed light on why suicidal thoughts and actions are not

God's will and how we can move past those thoughts and actions into a life lived abundantly.

The first thing I want you to remember is that "God so loved the world that He gave His one and only Son, that whoever believes in Him shall not perish but have eternal life" (John 3:16, NIV). Make sure you get this. God loves you so much that He sent His only Son, Jesus, to die for you so that you can live forever if you believe in Him. My limited understanding of this scripture was my first error. I believed in Jesus, but I failed to acknowledge how much God really loved me. God loved me so much that He sent His Son to die for me! That's some kind of love! To even think about taking my own life was selfish. I felt unloved because I failed to recognize the One who loved me first, the One who went to great lengths so I could live eternally with Him.

This is evidence that our lives matter to God. The sooner you realize this truth, the sooner you can shift to a mindset of pleasing God even when you feel worthless. Making a decision to live pleases God. If this applies to you right now, remember that God loves you in a way that is greater than your level of comprehension concerning love. Let His love be enough for you. His love is more than you could ever expect from anyone anyway (Romans 8:35–39).

God's love for us is demonstrated in too many ways to name in this setting. Knowing that He chooses us despite our shortcomings, forgives us every time we sincerely ask, and continues to pour His love on us daily is overwhelming. But what about how we love? The first thing that comes to mind is how we love others and how we treat others. Yes, we are commanded to love others. As a matter of fact, the second greatest commandment teaches us to love our neighbors as we love ourselves (Matthew 22:36–39). What we cannot afford to miss in this scripture, though, is the part that says "as you love yourself." This is evidence that one of God's expectations is that we love ourselves. To love is to have a feeling of strong or constant affection for a person, in this case for yourself. Notice the words *strong* and *constant affection*. We, being God's creations, are expected to have secure and unchanging feelings of care and fondness toward ourselves, which by God's design will successfully eliminate any desires to harm ourselves. So not only did I fail to acknowledge how much God loves me but I also missed the part where I was supposed to love myself. No matter how hard I tried to love others, I still disobeyed God's command by forgetting His expectation for me to love myself.

Young man, we are fearfully and wonderfully made (Psalm 139:14). God plans to prosper you and give you hope and a future (Jeremiah 29:11). We are His workmanship (Ephesians 2:10), created in His image (Genesis 1:27). He who began a great work in you will bring it to completion (Philippians 1:6). You were created by love because God is love (1 John 4:8), so love yourself and experience the fullness (at least what we are able to comprehend) of God's love for you.

As I grew older and became closer to God, my understanding of the importance of love also grew. I started to reflect more on the price Jesus paid for me so that I might live. You see, Jesus died for me. The price was His life. He took on *all* of my (and your) sins, nailing them to the cross and canceling our debt, which condemned us (Colossians 2:13–14). This is what separates Him from others who have given their lives. Only He, the perfect Lamb, could be our sacrifice. He died so that I could one day be reunited with Him in perfection.

Young man, let me share a practical example with you. At some point in our lives, we all will purchase or buy something. I don't purchase anything unless I really want it or need it. If it costs a lot and I still choose to purchase it, I'm going to take really good care of it. To take this a step further, if I lend someone something that costs me a lot, I expect that person to take supreme care of it while it is in their possession. For example, if a friend or family member asks to borrow my car, I expect them to take exceptional care of it and to be extremely careful while driving it. I would do the same thing if I borrowed someone's car because it doesn't belong to me and because it's of value to them. Well, scripture teaches us that our bodies are temples of the Holy Spirit, who is in us, whom we have received from God, and that we are not our own but were bought with a price (1 Corinthians 6:19–20). So each one of us belongs to God; your life, young man, was purchased by God with the payment of Jesus's perfect life, and your body is where the Holy

Spirit desires to dwell. In order for His Spirit to dwell in you, my young brother, you must live and not die!

Now knowing all of this, how do you think God (the Father, Son, and Holy Spirit) expects you to handle this life and body that you have been given while here on earth? Your life and your body should be your sacrifice to Him, who created you and who loves you more than any other (Romans 12:1).

We do not own ourselves, so we must handle that which belongs to God with care. When attempting to commit suicide, I was ignorant of the fact that my life is not my own. I belonged to God then, and even now, twenty-plus years later, I am still totally His. Harming myself purposely is not how God wanted me to treat one of His most precious possessions. (And yes, I am precious to Him, and so are you: "You shall be a crown of beauty in the hand of the Lord, and a royal diadem in the hand of your God" [Isaiah 62:3, ESV].) Jesus has authority over me and rights to the life I live and the body in which my being is housed. Shame on me for treating His treasured creation, a creation that cost greatly, like it had no value! Thank God I am forgiven.

With growth in Christ comes understanding. The more we spend quality time with God reading His Word, praying, and meditating, the more we will begin to love as He intended. We will begin to look at ourselves and see how uniquely God created us and start to seek His purpose for our lives. "For we are His workmanship [His own master work, a work of art], created in Christ Jesus [reborn from above—spiritually transformed, renewed, ready to be used] for good works, which God prepared [for us] beforehand [taking paths which He set], so that we would walk in them [living the good life which He prearranged and made ready for us]" (Ephesians 2:10, AMP). Your life has purpose. Loving yourself enough to seek God for that purpose is only the beginning of a beautiful journey toward Heaven.

On this journey everything you need will be given to you by God the Father, who graciously gives us all things (Philippians 4:19, Romans 8:32). Yes, all things. Young brother, you can be confident that anything you ask according to God's will is yours (1 John 5:14–15). You need only to confess with your mouth that Jesus is Lord and believe in your heart that God raised Him from the dead (Romans 10:9). Then life can be lived through Him abundantly. Receive Him as your gift today.

Chapter 2

HAPPY BIRTHDAY

Birthdays are arguably the most celebrated milestones in the human life span. It's not only a day that we celebrate our birth but it's a day when others celebrate us as well. Birthday well-wishes from fathers, mothers, siblings, cousins, friends, and associates are common. Then there is the birthday party, which, for some, may happen every year. For others, however, certain birthdays may hold more importance, prompting the party to happen every five years or so. Parents value each birthday their children are blessed to see. However, the first, third, and fifth birthdays are special. So are the tenth and sixteenth birthdays, when some parents are willing to break the bank to make their children happy. Sixteen is so special that society decided not to mention it without putting the word *sweet* before it. What about the good old eighteenth birthday? In our culture most people consider themselves grown at eighteen. They often do grown-person things and have grown-people kind of fun to celebrate. Reminding others that they are grown becomes their favorite thing to say. I'm sure you have heard someone say this before: "I'm a grown man!"

Regardless of how it's celebrated, all birthdays are valued by most individuals. It's another year of life, a new you. Even my young son, who is not even ten years old yet, instantly feels worthy and better about himself with each new year of life. Sometimes he reminds me by saying, "Daddy, I'm not a baby anymore. I'm seven!" He says it as if I should know that he is more mature now than in previous years. Then there is this idea of him attempting to be more independent and showing his mom and me how much he has grown over the years. Though this may be true, he still doesn't mind climbing into our bed at night in order to fall asleep.

As a child I thought birthday parties were the best. It didn't matter whether it was at the person's house or if their parents rented out a place for them to have it. It was a party! I didn't experience many of my own birthday parties, but I got invited to a lot, and that fueled my desire for one of my own. I wanted that feeling of being showered with love from friends; being flooded with gifts, cards, and money;

and being the center of attention for a few hours. I wanted people to celebrate me and sing to me for my birthday. I wanted everyone to acknowledge that I was a year older and that I was worthy of a birthday party.

So at nine years old, I asked my parents to throw me a party for my tenth birthday. I didn't just ask for a party though. I was specific with them, and I asked them for a pool party at the local pool. Now this meant that they would have to plan for this party. They would have to plan the date, time, and financial budget for the party. Although it was not my first time asking for a party, I knew that eventually I would get what I asked for as long as it was within my parents' budget and was what they wanted for me. So after nine long years, I had a birthday party—a big birthday party at the local swimming pool for my tenth birthday. Boy, oh boy! It checked all the boxes. I was on cloud nine, and nothing or no one could bring me down. I felt loved, valued, favored, important, cool, and blessed. It was exactly what I wanted, and the wait was well worth it. After years of seeing everyone else have parties and be showered with love on their birthday, it was finally my time. My parents had come through in a major way.

My "birthday high" lasted for a few days; then it was back to normal. I was still happy that I actually had a party, but the overwhelming joy of that day faded. That joy was something that I wished I could experience every day instead of having to wait a whole year to have another chance at experiencing it. Wouldn't that be something? A birthday celebration every day? I wonder how much happier people would be if they felt loved every day, valued every day, important every day, and like they mattered every day. I'm sure it would make a big difference in the way we approach life and the decisions we make.

Every day, however, cannot be all about us. We have to share special moments and celebrate others as well. That's what makes birthdays so special. It's the fact that they don't happen every day, giving everyone a chance to feel loved, important, blessed, and favored, even if it is only once a year...right?

Well, I'm going to argue that birthday celebrations can, do, and should happen every day. The problem is, young man, that we sometimes don't even show up for our own party. I know some of you are thinking, "What in the world is he talking about?" but stay with me for a minute. Let me speak first to those of you who have already accepted Jesus Christ as your Lord and Savior. The moment that you accepted Him, the angels in Heaven rejoiced and celebrated the new you. You became a new creature, a better one than you were the moment before. You were reborn—you had a birthday. On this birthday the old you (last year's you) died, and the new you was alive in God through Christ Jesus (Romans 6). That was your moment! God and the angels were happy for you, and you were instantly surrounded with love. You were the center of attention, and a long list of gifts were given to you, the most important gift being eternal life. Since you invited God into your heart to party with you, He instantly put you on the VIP list for His house party in Heaven. Remember the joy you felt in that moment? Some of you were so happy you may have cried. Others may have felt like it was the best day of your life. Some of you were so overwhelmed that you passed out and hit the floor. Regardless, we should always remember that very special birthday, and each day, we should walk in the joy of that day so that our zest does not fade.

Each day should be like a birthday as we recommit, turn away from sin, and meet with and surrender to Christ daily. How often, though, do we do this? How often are we seeking Him and His presence? This is what I mean when I say, "We sometimes don't even show up for our own party." Think about it. God invites us to meet with Him (party with Him) every day, multiple times a day if we desire, and every day He brings us gifts. What gifts? Life, health, strength, and brand-new mercies to name a few. He brings us gifts we didn't even have to ask for, gifts He knows we need. However, we miss out on certain gifts simply because we don't show up to receive them.

Consider the times you felt anxious, nervous, or afraid when faced with a situation, and you didn't consult or spend time with God before facing it. It is possible that you didn't have peace or the courage you needed because you didn't show up to get your daily gift from the One who keeps on giving like it's your birthday. Christ wants you to feel like you're on cloud nine each and every day. He wants you to feel showered with love and flooded with gifts. He even rejoices and sings over you (Zephaniah 3:17). Showing up and meeting with Him daily makes it possible not only to feel valued but also to feel the joy that comes with His presence. Consider each day a gift, and allow each experience with God to keep you feeling special because you are.

If you are reading this and you have not invited Jesus Christ into your heart to be your Lord and Savior, then the best birthday of your life still awaits you. Jesus, the guest of honor, is just waiting for His invitation so that He can give you a gift that only He can give. Because of His unconditional love for you, He gives you gifts daily. But you have yet to unwrap the greatest gift that you could ever receive. That gift is eternal life (Romans 6:23).

The cool thing is you don't have to wait days, months, or a full year to experience this birthday. There is no special time or place required to make this birthday special. "If you declare with your mouth, 'Jesus is Lord,' and believe in your heart that God raised him from the dead, you will be saved. For it is with your heart that you believe and are justified, and it is with your mouth that you profess your faith and are saved" (Romans 10:9–10, NIV). All you have to do is invite Him in. If you are ready, say this prayer with me:

Jesus, I know that I am a sinner, and I ask for Your forgiveness. I believe that You died on the cross for my sins and that God raised You from the dead. I turn away from my sins and invite You to come into my heart and life. I want to trust and follow You as my Lord and Savior. In Your name, amen.

Happy birthday, young man! I join the angels in Heaven in celebrating you in this moment. I urge you now to spend time with God on a daily basis and seek to know His ways so that you can start living a life that represents Christ. Don't get complacent with your confession. Instead invite Jesus into your heart every day, and always keep Him on your mind.

Chapter 3

LIVE WITH INTEGRITY

What I would like to do now is focus on a character trait that I believe is the key to living a choice-filled life in Christ Jesus. That character trait is integrity. Some of you may or may not know exactly what integrity is, but in its simplest form, integrity is doing the right thing, no matter what. That is the easiest way to remember what integrity is. However, I would like to go a little deeper into this character trait. I'm going to give you three different definitions of integrity, and I'm going to zoom in on certain words that make up each definition so that you are better equipped to live a life of integrity starting today.

INTEGRITY IS THE QUALITY OF BEING HONEST AND HAVING MORAL PRINCIPLES
(dictionary.cambridge.org)

Now having moral principles simply means that you have a good foundation of beliefs regarding what is right or wrong. But the word that I would like us to zoom in on right now is the word *honest. Honest* means "to be free of deceit and untruthfulness" (lexico.com). Many times an honest person is described as someone who tells the truth or someone who will tell you what they really feel or believe—someone you can count on to keep it real with you. While that may be accurate, an honest person is also true to who they are and is committed to their life values and beliefs. So let's go back to this definition. Integrity is the quality of being honest. *Honest* means to be free of deceit and untruthfulness. So if *honest* means to be free, then deceit and untruthfulness hold you captive from being who you really are. Deceit and untruthfulness hold you back and keep you from being the best version of yourself. You were born to be great, with a specific purpose. You were made to be great *as you.* The only thing that can prevent that from happening is the practice of being who you are not supposed to be, which is being dishonest to who you really are, which is the equivalent of living with a lack of integrity.

Gangster rap was my choice of music in the early 1990s. I would rap every word to songs, some of which I knew were inappropriate in relation to my faith. It didn't matter how bad the language in the song was; if I liked the song, I would rap along. I idolized certain rappers and tried to personify the things they were rapping about. When Snoop Doggy Dogg dropped his *Doggystyle* album, I thought he was the coolest rapper and person on the face of the earth. He had a certain charisma and a certain swag that was just cool to me. There was a coolness to the way he rapped his lyrics. If only you could have heard me trying to transform my Southern accent to match his West Coast one. Nobody could tell me that I didn't sound cool like Snoop. Because of Snoop, I wanted to trade my sixth-grade wardrobe for a pair of Chuck Taylors and a blue, khaki suit or Dickies suit. That had become cool gear. It's what gangstas wore, and I wanted to be one. Again, I was in the sixth grade. My parents weren't raising no gangsta.

To tell the truth, I knew that I had already committed to a different lifestyle, and deep down inside, I knew God was not pleased with me. But I wanted to fit in. I wanted to be accepted in my imperfect neighborhood. The problem, however, was who I was trying to be didn't match up with who I really was. The real me was president of the student body at school, the real me was in band and chorus, the real me was compassionate—too compassionate to be a gangsta. And oh yeah, I was saved—I just wasn't acting like it.

See, I knew Jesus but denied Him with my actions. Perhaps that is you today: giving glory in front of your church family but giving gangsta to your peers. Praising on Sunday, perpetrating on Monday. I'm only saying this because I have been there. Know this though. As much as Jesus loves you, He does not want you lukewarm (Revelation 3:15–16). Don't straddle the fence! Be all in with Christ, and He will welcome you with outstretched arms. Young man, we gotta make it to Heaven. Your reward for walking with Christ awaits you. It doesn't matter how old you are; commit today to live a life worthy of the call. For you have been called by God (Ephesians 4:1).

I lacked integrity because I wasn't being my true self. I know that I was young and in the sixth grade, but I missed out on being the greatest me that I could be at that time for trying to be Snoop. Only Snoop could be great as Snoop, and I should have been being great as Decius. I was a leader and a pretty good trumpet player, and I could really sing. I was also really good at baseball. I should have been trying to be great at those things because that is who I was. Instead I wasted a lot of time trying to be something else, trying to be something that took way too much effort. What I'm saying is don't lie to yourself about who you are and who you know you should be. I'm also saying don't live a lie or tell one just so other people will accept you. I'm saying be honestly you. Be true to yourself. Be free. For you are fearfully and wonderfully made (Psalm 139:13–16).

INTEGRITY IS FIRM ADHERENCE TO A CODE (SYSTEM OF RULES) OF MORAL VALUES
(merriam-webster.com)

A code is a structure. It's how something is set up; it's a method of doing things, an approach or practice. Young man, what kind of code do you adhere to? What is your method of doing things in life? What rules do you live by? I only ask because in order to be a person of integrity and a true representation of Christ, these are all questions you must ask yourself. What are your rules for living? Rev. Dr. Martin Luther King Jr. asked it this way: "What is the blueprint of your life?" Once you have answered these questions, you must then evaluate your answers to make sure that they are in alignment with integrity and living a life that is Christ centered.

You don't reach integrity by lying and cheating. You don't reach integrity by following the crowd. You don't reach integrity by trying to be something that you're not. These things are not in alignment with how Christ wants us to live. You reach integrity when you live by the code of "Do the right thing, even when nobody is watching." You reach integrity when you practice telling the truth, even when it's hard to do so. You reach integrity when you decide to be real and not fake. You reach integrity when what is right becomes more important than what is easy. How are you practicing to be a person of integrity? What code do you live by?

You ever wonder why doing the wrong thing is so easy? Think about it. It's easy to do the wrong thing, but doing the right thing can be hard sometimes. Why does the pull of the world or non-Christian behavior seem to be so much stronger than the pull of being Christlike? There must be some good that comes from doing the right thing. Satan wants you to be on the wrong side of right for a reason. It's easy to make excuses about why you don't read your Bible, but there is a reward that comes with understanding scripture. It's easy to just cheat and get what you want, but there's a reward that comes with earning things honestly. It's easy to tell that lie. As a matter of fact, a lie is the first thing that comes to mind when faced with a situation in which a negative consequence might be attached.

Here's the thing though: people of integrity accept consequences as opportunities for growth. So the next time you think about telling that lie, think about whether it's going to help you grow. Think about whether it's going to help you make it to Heaven. Think about what Jesus would do. What code do you live by?

People follow certain codes all the time. It seems that worldly codes have the greatest effect on young men these days. When we see, hear, or know that something wrong has happened, the "no snitching" code takes precedence. I understand that there are reasons for this, but I'm amazed at how committed people have become to this code even when fear isn't the concern. Gangs live by certain codes, and some members would rather die than break them. That's some commitment. Here is what I believe though. I believe that if every man, no matter how young or old, who has accepted Jesus Christ as his Savior would commit to the code that Jesus has laid out for us, together we could change the world. There is no doubt in my mind. If we were as loyal to Christ as some are to their street gangs, we would see a change in our communities and schools. Some street gangs even recruit in order to make their gang stronger. What if we did that? What if we were so in love with Christ that we recruited people to join our Heaven-bound gang? What if our daily objective was to make the body of Christ stronger?

Young man, as I reflect, I realize that after accepting Christ at nine years old, God always placed me in positions of influence. He set the stage for me to introduce others to Him. He allowed me to be voted student body president in sixth grade. I was the starting point guard and starting quarterback in junior high school—all positions of influence. When I was in high school, I had the opportunity to put Christ on full display as one of the most popular students in the entire school. I was the star quarterback of the varsity football team, an all-star baseball player, a member of the Student Government Association, and a peer mediator.

However, I missed the opportunity to make the body of Christ stronger because I lacked integrity. I mean, really! There I was with arguably the biggest platforms that the average student could have. Allowing God to use me then would have been amazing. I failed Him miserably by using those positions to bask in my own glory. I wasn't being who

I knew God had called me to be. I consistently broke God's code for my life and followed a worldly one in order to please myself and appeal to my peers.

It wasn't until the end of my senior year of high school that I decided to rededicate my life to Christ and get more serious about my faith, but at that point, my peers weren't really vibing with my change. While some were happy for me, others took advantage of the opportunity to tease me about not being able to have sex anymore. I wanted others to see that being saved was actually cool, but it seemed the opposite was happening. What if I had not taken God's grace for granted? What if I had never turned my back on God? How much more of an impact could I have made in the lives of my peers? I could have still been cool, popular, athletic, and saved. I could have really influenced my peers to give Jesus a try.

Now I'm telling you all of this for a reason. I'm telling you this because you—yes, you—have the opportunity to make an impact for Christ from whatever platform you have, and I don't want you to miss it. Those years of my life would have been much better if I were more focused on making it to Heaven and allowing Christ to be on full display in my life in order to enhance His kingdom. Instead of putting Him on display, I either tried to hide Him or only let Him show when it was convenient.

Living by a code can be a good thing, but it must be the right code. One day we will leave this earth, and when we do, young man, I want the code that we live by to be known by all. For God I live, and for God I'll die (Romans 14:8). That's my code. What's yours?

INTEGRITY IS AN UNIMPAIRED (NOT WEAKENED OR DAMAGED) CONDITION
(merriam-webster.com)

There will be situations and outside influences that will challenge your integrity at times. But a person of integrity must not be weakened or broken by these situations and influences. The world has a way of drawing us into negative behavior and making us think that what is wrong is actually right. TV shows and social media platforms have enlightened us to behaviors that are not of God, but wide acceptance of these behaviors has managed to cloud our judgment. However, we should not conform to the world. We should renew our minds so that we will know what God's will is (Romans 12:2). If we take the world's view on things, we will find ourselves on the wrong side of right when our integrity is challenged. Let me give you some examples of when your integrity might be challenged:

- You're leaving the store, and you realize that the person at checkout gave you twenty dollars back instead of five dollars.
- You see a woman digging in her purse, and a one-hundred-dollar bill drops out when she doesn't realize it.
- A young lady asks you to come over to her house because she is home alone.

- You are asked to participate in something that everybody else is doing, but you know it's not right.

I know that I don't have to tell you what a person who is trying to make it to Heaven should do in these situations. I will tell you this though. Sometimes choosing Christ won't be the most popular decision. People who choose Christ often stand with few and are not afraid to stand alone (2 Corinthians 6:17). Having integrity will require you to be strong, but when that time comes, just refer to the code that you want to live by and do it. Commit to it, and let nothing or no one tempt you to go against it. Be free! Be honestly you, and always remember Jesus.

I urge you to start thinking of things from a perspective of Heaven and Hell. When your integrity is challenged, when you feel like acting out of character, when you get upset and violence becomes an option, when lying is what seems easy, when telling the truth is difficult, and when you're tired of being nice, think about whether your decision in those moments will draw you closer to Heaven or Hell. Set your heart and mind on things above so that when Christ appears, you will also appear with Him in glory (Colossians 3:1–14).

Chapter 4

BECAUSE I SAID SO

My parents took great care of me as a child. All my needs were met, and more than enough of my desires were granted because they obviously loved me. I have many good memories from my youth, but I still couldn't wait to get out of my parents' house. It just seemed like growing up and being on my own was taking forever to become a reality. I wanted to come and go as I pleased. I was tired of having to do chores; I was tired of being told what to do, which sometimes happened without explanation. I couldn't wait to be grown so I could do me.

Young man, I bet you heard these words before: "As long as you live in this house, under this roof, you're gonna abide by my rules and do what I tell you to do." Yep, I heard that a lot. The problem was there were some things my parents would tell me to do that just didn't make sense to me. All right, here's an example. My dad would be watching TV in the family room, and he would yell for me to come to him from the other side of the house. I would rush to him (at first), thinking something serious had happened. I would enter the family room, only to hear him say to me, "Hand me the remote from the table." What's so bad about that? you may ask. Well, *the remote would only be five feet away from him.* Was I his personal servant? That worked my nerves.

Here's another example. Sometimes I would ask to go bike riding with my friends from the neighborhood. If I was allowed to participate, I was told that I could only ride up and down our street. Yep, you read that correctly—I was only allowed to ride on the street that I lived, which was the length of a football field. Please understand that my friends were not planning to only ride on my street. Who wants to be limited to just one street for bike riding? Even now I don't see how my parents thought that was cool.

There were also times when I was told to do things, and if I felt big and bad enough on that day, I would ask the question every child wants to know: why? Most times I thought it was a fair question. I felt I had a right to know. Why? Why do I have to do this? Why do I have to do that? Nothing's wrong with that, right? I assume my parents had a slightly different point of view though. See, they didn't think that they owed me an explanation. Therefore, my "why" was often met with the response "Because I said so!" Hearing that response irritated me more than anything. One time I remember being so annoyed after hearing it that I vowed that if my children (if I had any in the future) ever asked me "why?" I would always explain to them my reasoning. I was not going to respond to them disrespectfully like my parents responded to me.

I can imagine that you feel me on this matter. Sometimes parents just don't seem to have the answers we need as young men, or they don't seem to value our perspectives enough to offer us well-thought-out explanations for our whys. Children are simply expected to obey, no questions asked. So believe me, I have been where you may be presently. You are no different from what I was in my youth—you can't wait to live life by your own rules. I get it. Even now as a grown man, I understand your frustration, although the passing years and fatherhood have positioned me to view this from a different perspective. Wait, stay with me, young man. Let me explain.

As children it is often difficult to see that parents not only have your best interest at heart but also know what is best for you. Your mom and your dad have walked many miles in your shoes, for they were once children too. They know the outcomes, challenges, and dangers that await you outside of their personal care. Your parents have been tasked to provide for you, to nurture you, to prepare you for life as an adult, and to protect you. (If you have ever been asked to babysit a younger sibling or little cousin, you should be able to relate on some level to what your parents do for you all the time.) Guys, that's a big job! And it is not easy.

Your parents are pressured every day to make the right decisions for their precious sons. Your mother and father are human; they have eyes and ears and fears, just like you. They see the boys and "grown" men who aren't making it. They hear the evening news reports of boys and men serving time in correctional institutions for crimes and bad decisions. In the newspapers or maybe on the internet these days, they read about the mother whose son is missing or the father who now advocates for suicide prevention. In their very own communities, they are watching boys be killed in cold blood. No parent wants these horrors for their boys. Yet these horrors (and more) await you, young man, at every turn and every corner, and your parents love you too much to throw you into the raging waters without a life jacket, knowing you can't swim.

Unfortunately, parents don't always make the right choices. And guess what, they don't always know the right answer. But still they must make constant judgments that will directly affect your future. They want you to make it, young man! Respect your parents and even their because-I-said-sos. Honor them because you realize that all they want is to raise a strong male child who succeeds in life. I share this with you because I know there is a promise attached to your humble obedience toward your parents, young man.

There are over thirty scriptures in the Bible about honoring and respecting your parents and elders. That's how important this is to God. Exodus 20:12 (ESV) reads, "Honor your father and your mother, that your days may be long in the land that the Lord your God is giving you."

I'm not saying that it is wrong or that it is a sin to ask why, but understand that the lack of an explanation or a reasonable answer does not mean that there is a lack of love or respect for you. As a parent myself, I want my son to trust me when I tell him to do something. I want him to trust that I would not tell him to do anything that would harm him. I want him to respect me and my love for him so much that when I ask him to do something, he will just do it. He will do it knowing that I, his daddy, would do anything within God's will for him. I'm sure my parents felt the same way. Sure, my parents used teachable moments to help me grow in character, and in those moments, they would provide explanations. Other times, though, they just wanted me to trust and respect them. They wanted me to show my love for them by being obedient. Now I'll be honest; I try not to use the response "Because I said so" with my son. Instead I choose to say, "Just do it," which I guess is pretty much the same thing.

How much different is this with God? How often do you ask God why or question the dos and don'ts regarding how He expects you to live? "God, why do I have to turn the other cheek? Why should I pray for my enemies? Why do I always have to be nice when others are not nice to me?" The answer to our questions may sometimes seem to go unanswered, or it may feel like God is simply saying, "Because I said so." As you grow in understanding of God's will for your life, some things may not seem fair. Some things may not even make sense to you. God, our Father, knows what's best though. He has our best interest at heart (Jeremiah 29:11), and He who knows all knows that things will work out in your favor if you obey Him (Romans 8:28). He sent His Son, Jesus, to walk in our shoes, and He knows the outcome of every challenge and situation we may face. As His children, who are we to question His reasoning or His directives? Believe in your heart that He is omnipotent, all-powerful; He is omnipresent, everywhere; and He is omniscient, all-knowing. When you believe these things about God, you will learn to trust Him, even when you don't understand.

When I think of obedience to God, I think of Abraham and his son Isaac, the Bible story found in Genesis 22 (NIV), starting at the second verse. Here is what it says:

> Then God said, "Take your son, your only son, whom you love—Isaac—and go to the region of Moriah. Sacrifice him there as a burnt offering on a mountain I will show you."

Yes, you read that correctly. God told Abraham to sacrifice his only son as a burnt offering and did not provide an explanation! This was probably a good time to stop everything and ask God why, right? I would argue that most parents would have pretended that they didn't hear God or find reasons to believe that it wasn't God speaking to them. However, Abraham's response was different. We learn in verses 3 through 18 that Abraham did not delay in doing what God told him to do. He gathered everything that he would need in order to sacrifice his son and started on his journey to the place that God told him about. Once they reached the place God had told him about, Abraham built an altar, arranged the wood, bound his son Isaac, and laid him on the altar, on top of the wood. He then took out his knife to slay his son, but the angel of the Lord called out to him from Heaven, telling him not to lay a hand on his son. God provided a ram instead for Abraham to sacrifice, and Abraham was blessed greatly for his obedience to God.

Now Abraham didn't question God because he trusted God to provide. He believed that God was omnipotent, omniscient, and omnipresent. Is it wrong to question God? Yes and no. It is okay to question Him for better understanding. He wants you to grow in understanding. It is not okay to question His will, decision, or purpose. When you do question Him with pure motives and He doesn't answer you, don't take His silence as disrespect. Understand that in His time, He will reveal all things to you.

God wants us to trust Him when He tells us to do something. He wants us to trust that He would not tell us to do anything that would bring us harm. He wants us to love Him so much that when He asks us to do something, we will just do it. We will do it, knowing that He, our Father, is able to do exceedingly and abundantly more than we can ask or think (Ephesians 3:20).

I understand that sometimes we all just want to know why. If you are asking God about something that baffles you, I have some good news. God does answer our whys in teachable moments. Let's hang out in the book of Proverbs 3:1–12. In this passage of scripture, each instruction given is followed by the reason we should follow the instruction, or the why. Here is how it is written in the New Living Translation:

- *Verse 1.* "My child, never forget the things I have taught you. Store my commands in your heart."
  Verse 2. "If you do this, you will live many years, and your life will be satisfying."
- *Verse 3.* "Never let loyalty and kindness leave you! Tie them around your neck as a reminder. Write them deep within your heart."
  Verse 4. Then you will find favor with both God and people, and you will earn a good reputation.
- *Verse 5.* "Trust in the Lord with all your heart; do not depend on your own understanding."
  Verse 6. "Seek His will in all you do, and He will show you which path to take."
- *Verse 7.* "Don't be impressed with your own wisdom. Instead, fear the Lord and turn away from evil."
  Verse 8. "Then you will have healing for your body and strength for your bones."

- *Verse 9.* "Honor the Lord with your wealth and with the best part of everything you produce."
  Verse 10. "Then He will fill your barns with grain, and your vats will overflow with good wine."
- *Verse 11.* "My child, don't reject the Lord's discipline, and don't be upset when He corrects you."
  Verse 12. "For the Lord corrects those He loves, just as a father corrects a child in whom he delights."

God wants us to show our love for Him by being obedient with or without explanation. However, He is the God who loves us enough to provide explanation of the reward that follows obedience. Let's make a commitment to obedience today, even when we don't understand the why. God knows the plans He has for us (Jeremiah 29:11), and obedience to Him is the way to our eternal reward. Go get it!

Chapter 5

THE MIRROR THAT DOES NOT LIE

Since I still have your attention, let me remind you that God loves you more than you can imagine. He loves you right now, wherever you are in Him, whatever you are dealing with in life, and however you feel about yourself. He loves you, young man!

Sometimes we reject God's love because we feel unworthy. We feel like we are not good enough at times, and we think that God is not really there for us because we sin so much. Have you ever felt like you don't have a chance at a real relationship with God because you have some sinful habits that you need to get rid of first? Well, if you answered yes to that question, I have good news for you. That's not true! God wants you right where you are, and He desires that you be in His will.

Self-awareness is defined as conscious knowledge of one's own character, feelings, motives, and desires. The idea of self-awareness comes from knowing exactly who you are and what you are capable of, be it good or bad. It's being honest with yourself so that you can be honest with others and with God about things that you want, things that you need, and things that you need to correct.

Young man, take a moment and look into a mirror, a full-body mirror if possible. What do you see? You see a reflection of yourself, correct? Are you satisfied with what you see? Did you, without even thinking, make an effort to fix something you didn't like about your image? Maybe you noticed you were slouching. Did you automatically stand up straight? You probably view this reflection every morning as you prepare for your day, right? How you perceive what you see in the mirror determines what you do next. If your hair is out of place in your opinion, you brush it so that it becomes pleasing to you. If your eyes are crusty and there is a drool line coming from your mouth, you wash your face so you look rested and refreshed for your peers and others you meet. You intentionally situate your clothing so that your swag is evident. Why do you take the time to do these things? You are invoking a physical self-awareness.

Subconsciously, you have an expectation of how you desire to appear physically. Therefore, you use the mirror—the reflection of your physical being—as a tool to self-correct. Your physical self-awareness enables you to self-evaluate and present an improved version of yourself based on your personal expectations for how you want to look. Interestingly, most of us do this every single day. We look in mirrors and make decisions. Yet sometimes we are negligent in our appearance, or depending on where we are going or what we are going to do, we don't care about our appearance. If we are making a quick run to the store, we might not even bother with our hair. If we are just going to work out, we figure, who cares about how we look, right?

There are places, however, where we have definite reasons to pull ourselves together because, to us, our image matters, like school, work, church, that party, or wherever the girls are chilling. These places of importance differ for different people. I'm from a small town in South Carolina. Walmart is where you see everybody—and I do mean everybody. Our Walmart services many towns that don't have their own. So a trip to Walmart mattered greatly to me as a young man. This was one of the places I had to represent.

Why don't we care about how we present ourselves all of the time though? It's possible that we have unconsciously placed a level of importance on certain places, events, and people. Why are we able to look into a mirror (and some-times we don't even bother to use the mirror), realize that we look a mess based on our own standards, and still com-fortably leave the house? When we do this, maybe we are saying that we don't care how others perceive us. Maybe we are saying that because we are not going anywhere special, it doesn't matter how we carry ourselves. Maybe the case is that we were rushed and did not have enough time to ade-quately present ourselves in a positive manner. Young man, are any of these your whys? Are you okay with this?

Moving from the physical to what I deem most import-ant, the spiritual, know this: self-awareness requires you to be in touch with your character, feelings, emotions, beliefs, doubts, desires, motives, and actions. (There is still a lot more to you than these listed.) And it absolutely requires you to be honest with yourself no matter what. Yes, self-awareness covers more than the physical you; it covers the whole you, including the part of you that is spiritual. Wait, you do real-ize that you are a spiritual being? Maybe you do, or maybe you don't. Or maybe your answer is yes—you know that you are a spiritual being, but you need clarity. Well, let me help you clearly understand. Once you accept Christ, His Spirit comes to dwell in you (Romans 8:9). And one of the Holy Spirit's roles is to help you become more like Christ. This involves taking on the spiritual attributes of Jesus.

What if you had a spiritual mirror—a mirror that you could peer into and see those things about you that don't line up with God's purpose for your life? How often would you use this mirror? Would you really be interested in allowing God, on a daily basis, to help you become who He designed you to be? Listen carefully to me, my young brothers: as men we cannot afford to ignore our spiritual selves. Spiritual self-awareness cannot be thrown out of the window. Spiritual self-awareness requires just as much intentionality and attention to detail as physical self-awareness. However, unlike physical self-awareness, spiritual self-awareness is directly connected to where you spend your eternity. Just like you have physical expectations for how you carry yourself, you must adhere to spiritual expectations that God has graciously given you. Spiritually, we have to take a good, honest look at ourselves, and just as we attempt to enhance our physical attributes, we have to be willing to better ourselves spiritually.

Christ followers must care about spiritual growth. To not care at all, or to care only at certain times or on certain occasions, is negligent on our behalf. No matter what we have planned for the day, giving attention to our spirit man must be a part of it. Even if you plan to sit in the house all day alone, check your spiritual mirror, not only before church, not only before going out with the pretty Christian girl you want to impress but also every day. Give attention to your spirit.

Okay, you understand by now that Christ followers should be spiritually healthy and that you must be intentional about paying attention to your spiritual man daily without fail. Looking into the mirror and seeing your physical reflection is simple enough, but on what standards do you base spiritual health? Where do you get a spiritual mirror? Young man, our spiritual mirror is the Word of God, which is found in the Bible (James 1:23–24). After accepting Christ as your Lord and Savior, you must build your spiritual man through the Word of God. "Faith comes by hearing, and hearing by the word of God" (Romans 10:17, NKJV).

Hold up, don't stop reading now. I get it. You have tried to read the Bible before, and you couldn't understand it because of all the *thous* and *yes*. However, there are various versions of the Bible made just for the young man. Now you may be wondering, "How do I use my spiritual mirror?" I'm glad that you asked because it's too important to leave out of your daily routine.

The Word of God allows us to see our true reflection, good or bad. Once we are honest with ourselves based on God's expectations, then we can begin the process of correction through the Holy Spirit's instruction. See, the Word of God is alive (1 Peter 1:23), so just reading it with an open heart allows it to live in you, and it therefore is working in you (1 Thessalonians 2:13). You will see yourself become more and more like Christ if you allow the Word of God to be your mirror. The Word of God is our guide for living. It's where we learn the attributes of Jesus so that we can live a life that reflects Him. The Word of God teaches us who we ought to be in Christ on a daily basis. You can live a pure life, young man, by obeying the Word of God (Psalm 119:9).

In order to obey God's Word, we must know what it says and seek to understand it. Therefore, we must read it and study it.

What does the Bible say about how we should love? There are many scriptures on love, but let's look at Romans 12:9–10 (CEV): "Be sincere in your love for others. Hate everything that is evil and hold tight to everything that is good. Love each other as brothers and sisters and honor others more than you do yourself." Have you loved others sincerely? Have you been honoring others more than yourself? This is a mirror moment that happens through the teachings of God's Word. You may be thinking that you don't even know where to begin or where to look in the Bible for certain things. Let me remind you that we live in a world in which technology is right at our fingertips. Google it! It's as simple as saying, "Hey, Google, what does the Bible say about _____?" And guess what, scriptures on the subject will pop up, allowing you to simply click the link or open your Bible and read.

Once we know what God's Word says about being followers of Christ, we can assess our spirit man using the mirror of truth. Need to assess your faith? There are scriptures for that. Need to know more about forgiveness? There are scriptures for that. What about the qualities of a Christian? There are scriptures for that too. All that we need for proper spiritual awareness can be found in our spiritual mirror. Once we spend time in that mirror, then we can reflect.

To reflect means to think deeply about something (collinsdictionary.com). Try reflecting on the previous day, weeks, months, or years, and think about the person you have been and areas in which you may need to improve in order to be the best version of yourself for Christ. Also, reflect on how patient God has been with you and how He continues to love you despite your wrongdoings and bad habits. How hard have you really tried to be right with God? This is your mirror moment! If you really desire a pleasing reflection, it won't take long for you to start pointing out your areas of growth and improvement. Reflect with the understanding that you will not be able to change things on your own, and many times you will need to spend time in the presence of your Helper.

We need a barber or a stylist for certain haircuts and hairstyles, and sometimes it may take a week or so before we can be worked in for an appointment. Sometimes we even walk in early in the morning, patiently waiting for a barber to have an opening, which could take hours. Depending on the hairstyle you desire, it could take months or even years for your hair to reach the desired length. However, if you want the haircut or hairstyle badly enough, you wait. While you wait, you continue to get tape-ups, twists, and braids to stay fresh. Well, during your reflection, it's important to remember that you need God for your spiritual touch-ups and makeovers. You must be willing to sit in His presence and wait on Him to help you through a true understanding of His Word. Whatever it takes, we have to take that good, hard look into our spiritual mirror so that we can evaluate our reflection and seek God to help us get in line with His will. If ever we find ourselves outside of His will, it's time to repent.

I want to ask you a question, young brother. How important is your spiritual reflection to you? How strong is your desire to reflect Christ in all that you do? I'm only asking because true repentance happens when your desire to reflect Christ in all things is a priority. To repent means to feel or express sincere regret or remorse about wrongdoing or sin. Biblically, however, repentance means more than just regret and remorse concerning sin. Repentance, according to our spiritual mirror, requires us to turn away from sin (Isaiah 55:7, Ezekiel 18:30–32). It requires that we have a change of heart, an inner change against sin and the world so that Christlike behavior may be produced.

You see, young man, without a change of heart toward sin, repentance is not sincere and becomes a formality of Christianity. We know that according to what Christians believe, we should repent and ask God to forgive us for our wrongdoing. That is the right thing to do, knowing that God will forgive us for all of our sins (Acts 3:19, 2 Chronicles 7:14). We have been conditioned, however, to feel just enough remorse and regret to bring us to our knees and ask for forgiveness, only to repeat the same cycles of sin, making what we think to be repentance a religious routine. We end up in the same cycles of sin because this routine causes us to seek His forgiveness more than we desire to reflect Him.

So you've read God's Word, reflected, repented, and prayed. It's common that you will feel better after doing these things since you spent time with God. I would argue, though, that remembering is often a forgotten ingredient. Praying can become routine (a good one, no doubt) and self-satisfying when done just because it's something that we know we should do often. Adding God's Word, reflection, repenting, and remembering to prayer, though, makes your prayer time intentional and gives you a higher chance of success when faced with opposition or temptation. Remember your time spent with God. Keep it at the forefront of your mind for the entire day. Remembering what we asked God to help us do will help us do it. This is how we recognize the power of our prayers in our daily lives. This is how we give God praise in the moment for answering even the little things. We remember what we asked for.

Remember, God's Word will never lie to you. When you look into your spiritual mirror, the reflection that you see is really you whether or not you like it or agree with it. Focus on aligning your reflection with the reflection of your Lord and Savior, Jesus; He is your example. The goal is to please the One who gave everything for you, and in pleasing Him, you are also securing your entrance into His eternal presence. Take some time each day to look into your spiritual mirror and attempt to present your best self to the world for Christ. You can do all things through Christ who strengthens you (Philippians 4:13).

Chapter 6

SAY WHAT?

I was blessed to have parents who believed in God and understood the importance of teaching their children how to live in a way that represents Him. They both exemplified godly characteristics in different ways, and my siblings and I were expected to follow their examples. They were active in our lives, so we had plenty of opportunities to observe, learn, err, and receive discipline. We learned to enjoy life, laugh, and love each other through game nights, family trips, sports events, outings with others, and daily mealtimes together. How we presented ourselves was a big deal to our parents. We were mandated, with very little room for error, to use good manners, be respectful, and control our language and tempers. But let me be real. We were children, so you already know we messed up sometimes.

In these moments I will never forget my mother's superspeed hand of discipline or, even worse, my father's lightning-quick response, "Say what?" If we ever heard Daddy say, "Say what?" I promise you everyone was correcting themselves whether they were the culprit or not because Daddy didn't play no disrespect or inappropriate language. Like I said, how we presented ourselves to others was important to my parents; they understood that our morals and language reflected who they were as parents. Because Mr. and Mrs. Jonathan Brown Jr. were ambassadors for God, their children were also expected to walk, talk, and act according to God's statutes. Listen, my parents were both public school educators, my dad was also a United Methodist pastor, and they both were positive citizens in our community. There was no room for negative reputations at our address. That was a definite no! And my siblings and I understood this clearly.

Now as far as I was concerned, I wasn't about to let the wrong thing get back to my parents. I didn't want to disappoint them, nor did I want the discipline that was sure to come with a negative report. As a young male, though, I was attracted to a lifestyle that did not match the one my parents taught me to live. So I did things on the low. When there was a threat to my parents' image around in the form of another adult, I was on my best behavior. When the threat was absent, however, there was no telling what I would do or say. I figured that everything was cool as long as my parents never found out.

As I wrote earlier, I was really into music in the 1990s, and gangsta rap was in full swing. I was all in, especially since I had a Walkman (a portable tape player) with headphones and didn't have to worry about my parents hearing what I was listening to. When I was in the sixth grade, I had a copy of Snoop Doggy Dogg's *Doggystyle* album, and I would listen to it every day. I easily learned every word to every song. I would rap the words while walking to school in the mornings and even during class sometimes. I would do this with any song that was out, if I liked it. Now gangsta rap had a lot of explicit language in it, and I was learning how to use that language really well.

Gangsta rap, however, was not the beginning of explicit language for me. Sadly, I was cursing long before I was into gangsta rap. My best friend often reminds me of how I cursed him out when we were in the fourth grade. I know— that's not something I'm proud of, but it's true. Needless to say, I used to curse. I did more than just curse a little; I cursed a lot. I might even go so far as to say that I had a cursing problem at one time. Cursing had become the best form of communication for me, especially if you could do it with some charisma, make people laugh, and make it sound good. It became natural to me, and that would continue to be the case for years. To me, I guess, what my parents couldn't see and hear wasn't hurting anything.

There were a few problems with my line of thinking. One, I was going against what my parents taught me. Two, I was painting a negative image for my peers when I should have been leading. Three, I was still claiming to be a follower of Christ, and I was not representing Him. During these years, I often felt guilty because of the inappropriate language I used. There were times that I felt really bad. However, that didn't stop me. What kind of person claims to be a follower of Christ but constantly speaks with worldly language?

The same question can be asked about all sin. How can we claim to be followers of Christ and constantly commit to sinful behavior? My parents would have been super disappointed if they had known. My heavenly Father, however, was listening to me and watching me the whole time. He knew everything. I imagine He was the one saying "say what?" to me when I was away from my parents, and I should have been correcting it quickly. I should have been living like I knew He was watching me because He was.

Allow me to share another short memory from my childhood. During the summertime, I would wake up with baseball on my mind. I couldn't wait to get outside with my glove and a tennis ball and work on my skills by throwing the ball against the brick wall of our house and catching it as many times as I could. I would play a nine-inning baseball game all by myself! I played every position. I was the pitcher, pretending there was a batter present. I was the umpire, calling balls, strikes, strikeouts, and walks. Some imaginary batters would reach first base by error, and others would hit home runs. I tried my very best to cleanly field every ball that I pretended was hit to me and to throw as many strikes as possible. The game always seemed to come down to the wire. I created climactic situations, feeling the pressure to win as if people depended on me and thousands were watching and cheering me on to victory from that brick wall. Though my performance in this major-league game really mattered to me, in reality, it was just me and the wall. Although nobody was really watching, I made every effort to be as close to perfect as I could be. My games against the wall eventually helped me become a better baseball player. All the strikes I threw and balls I fielded made for a smooth transition to the actual baseball field where I played on one of the community's recreational teams. Most importantly, I felt better prepared for some of the climactic moments that arise within a good game and game-changing situations that I faced on the field since I had already practiced them over and over again against the wall.

Former basketball player and UCLA basketball coach John Wooden once said, "The true test of a man's character is what he does when no one is watching." As young men we must do everything with purpose. In baseball, batters are taught to keep their eyes on the ball. In this Christian journey, we must keep our eyes on our purpose, which is found in Christ Jesus, who is in God and is God.

Young man, the goal is Heaven. Do not become complacent or satisfied with where you are on your walk. There will always be room for more growth. Pretending that thousands are always watching may be a good start for you in your journey to becoming more like Christ as it was for me in my baseball games against the wall. Each day is an opportunity to reflect Christ so that those who are watching may see Him in you. If we make representing Christ a daily practice in all that we say and do, then when life presents us with challenges and people are really watching, we have a better chance of allowing Christ to show in us. Our practice will translate into real-life application.

Satan wants you to fail. He wants you to mess up. He wants you to fall. He wants everyone to see you lose the race. He doesn't want you to influence anyone to follow Christ. But be encouraged! You can do all things through Christ who strengthens you (Philippians 4:13). Resist the devil, and he will flee from you (James 4:7). Remember that someone is watching you. You owe it to Christ to let your light shine so that others may see it and choose to follow Him (Matthew 5:16).

I could make every excuse in the world about my verbal vulgarity during this period in my life. I could say, "Well, I was young then." I could say, "Well, that's just what boys do." I could say I was just immature. I could even say that everybody curses a little when they're away from their parents. However, my goal here is not to make excuses. My goal is to liberate some young man who may be reading this with my truth. So here it is.

I was a young man who cared more about doing things that appealed to my peers and using language that made me sound cool than I cared about representing Christ, to whom I claimed I had surrendered my life. Understand it wasn't just the language I was using but also how I used the language. I was talking down to people, degrading females, using threatening language—language that promoted sexual immorality. It was wrong of me to speak this way, and I showed a lack of self-control. I should have been building people up and speaking against the very things I conformed to (Ephesians 4:29, Colossians 3:8, Titus 2:6–7, 12).

Don't get this twisted! We cannot willingly yield to sin over and over again and say that our truest desire is to please God (1 John 3:6). Nor do we continue to sin so that God's grace may increase (Romans 6:1). Instead, young man, we must practice Christlike behavior so that sin happens as a result of human imperfection and not deliberate disobedience. When we choose sin, we place hurdles in our path for the future. Some of those hurdles may be small and easy to overcome, but others may be ones that you trip over many times and struggle to conquer. The choices I made to continuously indulge in sinful behavior were more like placing mountains in my future path. Those mountains were impossible to conquer on my own but moved with much prayer and God's help. I encourage you today to be strong, young man. My actions were simply a display of my weakness, but my weakness was a faulty relationship with Christ. Therefore, be strong in the Lord and in His mighty power (Ephesians 6:10). This is not something that we are able to do on our own. This is something Christ does for us. Christ makes us strong!

People should be able to recognize Christ within us even more than they are able to recognize how our earthly parents are raising us. Let's be intentional, young man, about what we say, how we say it, and what we do. Let's do our best to reflect Christ and to be a good representation of the household of faith that we come from. Remember, our heavenly Father is always watching and listening.

PUT YOUR PRIDE ASIDE

I arrived at Claflin University for freshman orientation week. My parents and one of my sisters helped me move into the high-rise dormitory and get all of my things situated. I knew my parents were proud of me. I was now a college student, and I was living Christ out loud. After helping me move in and complete registration, they embraced me tightly, and we said our goodbyes. I remember the lump in my throat as I fought back tears and watched them walk away. Once I went back to my room and closed the door, it hit me. I was on my own, and that was a lonely feeling. I was alone in that dorm room for one week, and I reminisced about home.

Two of my female friends from Lake City were freshmen there as well. Early on we did everything together. We met other people and would hang out with them from time to time, but it was mostly just us during orientation week. One of our favorite things to do was hang out in the game room. We would shoot pool and play cards all the time; we played spades to be exact. We normally teamed up to play other people, but one day in particular, I teamed up with another freshman I met. We had a good game going, but my teammate and I were losing. To add salt to the wound, I made a costly mistake and took my eyes off the card table momentarily. Because of this I didn't know who played what card, and instead of disregarding what my partner might have played, I played a low card in case he had already won the hand. My friends won that hand, and my teammate was furious with me. Now my teammate and I were cool with each other, so I wasn't expecting his wrath. He cursed me out as if I were the worst partner he had ever had.

Pause! I know I was saved and all, but it had been a while since I had been faced with a situation in which I felt so disrespected. It had only been a few months since I rededicated my life to Christ, and I never felt the need to defend myself since doing so. Needless to say, before he could finish, I was giving him the same disrespect he was giving me. To add to that, I was ready to fight. My Christ switch had been turned off so easily. Maybe it was a test of my character or a moment that needed to happen to keep me humble, but whatever it was, I failed miserably. My walk with Christ changed after that.

No more Mr. Nice Guy! Time-out for representing Christ; I first needed to let everybody know that I wasn't some pushover. I wasn't a punk! I could curse, I could fight, and I wasn't afraid. Just like that, I no longer wanted to carry my cross. I would just pick it up later. I put my walk with Christ on hold. I was in a new place with new people, and their first impression of me couldn't be that I was soft. What will people back home think of me? Some of my closest friends were still in the streets, and I knew that they wouldn't approve of me being soft, even if I was saved. There was no room for that. At least that's how I felt. Perhaps this was a time when using my spiritual mirror would have helped, maybe some reflecting, repenting, and some praying too. Using my spiritual mirror would have reminded me that I have taken off my old self and its practices and have put on a new self (Colossians 3:9–10). It would have reminded me to be slow to speak and slow to anger (James 1:19–20). It would have reminded me to have nothing to do with foolish and stupid arguments because the Lord's servant must not quarrel (2 Timothy 2:23–26).

We must remember who we represent and not what we used to represent. We must remember who we are and let go of who we were before Christ came into our lives. Young man, during a game of spades, I allowed my pride and a desire to hold on to a pre-Christ reputation to cause me to discard my cross. Feeling disrespected caused me to forget about representing Christ in order to satisfy myself and not feel like less of a man. But that is exactly what representing Christ requires.

In order to represent Christ, we have to deny ourselves and commit to being less of who we naturally are so that Christ can manifest in us. Since we no longer belong to the world but to Christ, we can no longer respond as the world responds. I get it. It's hard to walk away or to just keep silent sometimes. But we must put our pride aside. The world has taught us to retaliate against any form of disrespect and to not let anyone talk to us in any kind of way. But the ways of the world lead us away from Christ and away from Heaven, young brother. Pleasing God is far more important than pleasing ourselves or others. I know it's difficult to not care about what other people will think, but God has the final say about the kind of life we have lived. God's judgment about our choices is all that matters.

Chapter 7

THE IMPORTANCE OF A TEAM

I learned at a very young age that you can't do everything by yourself. I learned that things get done a lot quicker and more efficiently when you have some help. My dad taught me this lesson on several occasions because he would recruit me almost every Saturday morning, when the weather was warm outside, to help him work in the yard. We had a decent-sized yard, front and back, and there always seemed to be something to do. We would tag team the grass when it needed to be cut, pull weeds from the cracks of the concrete in our driveway, rake and bag leaves, and do other things.

Yard work was not my favorite thing to do. I didn't understand why I always had to help out in the yard. I thought maybe that was a way for him to be mean to me because yard work is hard work; not only that but it was also really hot outside. My friends would be out riding bikes and playing, but I had yard work to do first. It just didn't seem right. There were times when my dad would make me work in the yard by myself. I remember wishing that he would come out and help because it felt like too much. I also wanted to get it done as quickly as possible so that I would have some daylight left to play outside with my friends.

At the time it didn't seem that there was a lesson to be learned or a benefit to me doing yard work. I know now, however, that my dad was not only teaching me how to be a hard worker but also teaching me the benefits of working as a team. When we worked as a team, the work we did was done quicker, we got more done with two people instead of just him or me working alone, and we always met the goal of making the yard look nice. My dad knew that he was able to work alone and get it done, but he also understood that doing it that way was not the most efficient way to do it. If he wanted to get more done in a shorter period, he would have to recruit some help, and that's exactly what he did. I'm sure he wanted me to see the value in having help when there is a lot of hard work to be done. That's why he allowed me to experience yard work with his help and without it. I would later learn to connect the dots from these teachings to other aspects of my life.

The hard work and the work-as-a-team mentality were, for me, easily transferred to the sports playing field. Outside of fundamentals, the one thing that my coaches would stress the most was the importance of playing as a team. They would say things like, "There is no I in team," and "We win and lose as a team." One of the most memorable things that I learned from sports was what the acronym TEAM means. T-E-A-M stands for Together Everyone Achieves More. It made perfect sense. What my dad was teaching me, everything my coaches were saying, it all made sense. There is no I in team, and we are better together. Together everyone achieves more. We won as a team, and when we lost, we lost as a team too. We were happy together when we won, and there were a lot of sad faces when we lost. In both experiences, though, there were lessons to be learned, and we learned those lessons as a team.

When learning to work as a team, there are some very specific things that must be done. In baseball, errors happen often. Teammates make mistakes when fielding ground balls and pop flies. Nobody is perfect. It happens to the best players. Since this is the case, you are taught in baseball to do what is called backing up your teammates. This simply means that whenever the ball is hit to a person, be it on the ground or in the air, someone else is responsible for being in a position to help in case that person misses the ball. Not only is this the case when the ball is hit to a teammate but it also is the case when the ball is thrown to a teammate. Teammates have each other's backs. That's a part of playing as a team. When teammates don't back each other up in baseball, an error in fielding might allow base runners to keep running and could also embarrass a teammate, lower a teammate's confidence, or make teammates feel that they have to do it on their own due to a lack of support. Once a teammate feels this way, the door is open for more errors to happen, and giving up on the game may become an option.

When trying out for a sports team, coaches look for players that can add value to the team. College athlete recruiters look to recruit players who can help take the school's athletic program to the next level and players who have their academic priorities together. Even at the professional level, teams look to draft players who have proved to be among the best at their position. Those are the players who they believe can help the team win a championship. A player's ability to add value to a team goes deeper than what their natural and physical attributes provide. Most prefer to add the kind of players who have good character and a team-first mentality and who know how to prioritize and balance life along with athletics. So many good players get left out because outside of their talent, they bring nothing to the table. It is important for scouts and recruiters to recognize this in a player because adding them to the team could be detrimental to the team's growth. Players also have to show that they bring more to the table than just physical talent. They must show that they can upgrade the team in other areas as well.

Young man, I want you to understand the importance of a team, but I also want you to understand the importance of building a team. For too long, young men (myself included) have been adding people to our circle and giving people positions in our lives that do not add any value to us. We have been adding people based on their talents alone and nothing deeper. We add people because they can give us a good laugh. We add people based on their status or popularity. We add some people out of fear. We fear them or their affiliations, so we see it as a benefit to add them to our circle. We add people based on race. We add people based on geographical location. We add people based on material things. Sometimes we even add people to our lives based on how they look. I could go on and on with this list. I could also make a pretty long list of why we choose not to add people to our team; I'm sure it would include many of the things listed above.

The bottom line is this. In order to maintain a Heaven-bound mindset, we need to be a part of a team with like-minded individuals on a consistent basis. We need teammates whose number one goal is Heaven. I'm not saying that having friends who are not there yet is a bad thing; maybe we can influence them to follow Christ. What I am saying, however, is this. If our team is full of people who do not have a Heaven-bound mindset, it could be detrimental to our growth in Christ.

Allow me to share another example from my childhood to make this clearer. I used to walk home after school since home was within walking distance for me in sixth grade. That was just another opportunity to be with the "in crowd." Of course, the in crowd were my friends at the time, and there would be ten to fifteen, sometimes more of us, walking home from school every day. I would learn a lot from hanging with this group of friends, mainly that knowing how to fight was a necessity. Even though my neighborhood was far from perfect, I didn't experience a whole lot of fighting growing up. Fights happened all the time in my neighborhood, but since my parents wouldn't allow me to go any further than one street in front of our house and the street behind it, I didn't see a lot of them.

Walking home was different though. Not only was I seeing fights happen often but I also was seeing my peers get jumped and beat up by multiple people at the same time. That was kind of new for me. I knew getting jumped was a thing, but I had never seen it happen firsthand, and now I had a front-row seat. I was terrified of getting jumped, but the idea of it fueled me to get tougher and more aggressive in case I had to fight. This was detrimental because at the tender age of nine years old, I had walked up to the front of the church during the altar call, or call to Christian discipleship as some of you may call it, and accepted Jesus Christ as my Lord and Savior. I prayed the Prayer of Salvation, asked Jesus to come into my heart, turned to the congregation, and announced that I was saved! Being saved meant that I had to love people, treat people with kindness, turn the other cheek, and stand up for what's right. It meant that I was to be a reflection of Jesus and that people should know I am His follower by the way I love others (John 13:35).

Developing this new tough-guy mentality, of course, caused me to drift further away from living a life that represented Christ. Instead of showing love and compassion toward others, I felt the need to harden myself to anything that would make me seem soft. I would also cling even closer to my friends whom I walked home with after school. When I got to junior high school (seventh and eighth grades), I was getting in fights after school for things as simple as someone stepping on my shoe. Like I said, I was drifting away from Christ, and the selection of my team contributed to that. It's not that they ever pressured me to fight or do anything wrong, but I felt the need to shift my persona to balance out the team. My mom would ask me if I had put Christ on the back burner. I would say no, but I'm sure she could tell that I wasn't putting Christ first in my life. I'm sure my peers didn't see much Christ in me during junior high school either. Those two years were tough for me. I smoked weed for the first time, lost my virginity, attempted suicide, and was embarrassingly disrespectful to my mom.

We decide the makeup of our team. We know if certain people are a good fit for us according to our goal of being more like Christ. Sure, I have friends who are not where I am spiritually. But I also have a team of people who can keep me lifted when this Christ walk gets difficult. I have teammates who add value to me, teammates who back me up with prayer and guidance when I make mistakes. I have teammates who help me keep my confidence in Christ Jesus when it feels like the enemy is winning. I have teammates who have their priorities in place, and their number one priority is Christ.

Once I realized the importance of a team while on this journey toward Heaven, the thought of facing my problems alone became a bitter memory. Why would I ever have chosen to face anything alone when I could have called for backup in my moments of despair. The time that I spent swimming lonely laps in my sorrows for feeling that I had failed God could have been a lot less tiring if I had the right teammates in position, reminding me that I am not perfect and that I am not alone. Understand that your team does not have to be big. Yes, a village is nice, but one or two solid teammates can be a huge help.

As I wrote in an earlier chapter, I rededicated my life to Christ toward the end of my senior year of high school. My girlfriend at the time accepted Christ as her Savior while we were dating. She, however, was representing Christ a lot better than I was then. I'm sure that I was a bad influence on her. But I remember her telling me, after she accepted Christ, that she knew I would be proud of her. I was very proud of her, and that could have been the push that I needed to be a better representation of Christ. Please consider this, young man: when choosing a girlfriend or significant other, they, too, are a part of your team and should add some spiritual value to your life. This is arguably someone who will absorb much of your time and attention and therefore should be someone who can help you grow in Christ instead of someone who stunts your growth in Him. There, I said it! So pray about her, then proceed according to God's will because no one is worth being outside of His will.

With a few months left in my senior year, my girlfriend took me to this play at a church one evening. The play was titled *Heaven's Gates, Hell's Fury.* As I sat back and watched different scenarios of people who were accepted into Heaven based on their belief in Christ Jesus and living a life that represented Him, I couldn't help but feel condemned by the scenarios in which people did not believe and did not represent Christ. Those people went to Hell. I believed, but I wasn't representing Christ. The mirror was before me, and I didn't like what I saw. It bothered me that I couldn't see myself as one who would enter Heaven's gates based on the scenarios that I saw. By the end of the play, I knew that I needed to surrender to Christ, but for some reason, I sat there contemplating, *Should I do it now? What will my friends think? Should I go home and pray first?* These questions were heavy on my mind. But when the pastor of the church grabbed the microphone and asked if there was anybody under the sound of his voice that wanted to be saved, I slipped my hand up, where only God could see it, and the pastor said, "I see you. Come on down from the balcony."

I made a decision to rededicate my life to Jesus Christ that evening. I felt secure. I had Heaven in my view. I had an overwhelming desire to be obedient to Him, and I was committed to walking in His will—so much so that I almost didn't attend my senior trip to the Bahamas with my fellow classmates. Not that I thought I was too good to go, but I knew my struggles and wanted to avoid the potential temptations that I might face. Being self-aware, I was conscious of some of the bad habits that I was fighting to break—sexual immorality being a major one for me. Such a short time ago, I had rededicated my life to Christ, and I didn't want to fail. I felt like I was walking into a lose-lose situation, and I felt that I would have to do it alone.

Still, I decided to go on the trip after learning that I could not get my deposit back. Moving with uncertainty of what God's will was for me could have been detrimental to my growth in Christ, but God showed me grace in the form of a friend. I expressed my concerns about the trip with her, and she encouraged me to go. She told me I would be fine and made a commitment to be my accountability partner. So I went on the trip and hung out with her for most of the time. I'm sure she sacrificed some of her own fun in order to keep me straight, but she did exactly what she said she would do. She held me accountable, and I was grateful for her friendship. Rest in peace, Farrah (Maxine) Turner (4/24/1982–10/22/2018).

The right teammates will remind us that the temptations we face are not uncommon to man (1 Corinthians 10:13). They are not ashamed to share with us their similar struggles and how they were able to overcome them. Even if they still struggle with your current struggle(s), there is beauty in holding each other accountable. When I fell into hitting slumps in baseball, my teammates were the ones throwing me extra batting practice in the batting cage. If we were both in a hitting slump, we threw each other extra pitches to help each other work our way out of the slump. We told each other what we were doing wrong, and sometimes we went back to the basics in order to help correct it. Those are the kinds of teammates we need on this journey to Heaven, the kinds that will point out what we are doing wrong and take the time to help us, even if that means going back to the basics, all in an effort to help us get better. Having those teammates in place will help us get to the next level in Christ.

The time is now, young man, to start building a team that you can win with. If you already have a team in place, build each other up and do the things that will help make your team stronger. Read your Bible together, repent and confess your sins to each other, pray for one another (James 5:16), and remember what you pray for. We face an opponent, Satan, who desires to destroy us. However, with teammates who have your back and Jesus as our coach, he cannot and will not win. In fact, he is already defeated.

Chapter 8

FLEE FROM IT

It is God's will that you should be sanctified: that you should avoid sexual immorality; that each of you should learn to control his own body in a way that is holy and honorable, not in passionate lust like the pagans, who do not know God; and that in this matter no one should wrong or take advantage of a brother or sister. The Lord will punish all those who commit such sins, as we told you and warned you before. For God did not call us to be impure, but to live a holy life. Therefore, anyone who rejects this instruction does not reject a human being but God, the very God who gives you his Holy Spirit.

—1 Thessalonians 4:3–8 (NIV)

I opened this chapter with a scripture because I understand that in today's society, sexual immorality is a sensitive topic in its various forms. So for the record, all that I write to you is according to God's law and His will for us. May all sensitive sinful issues be taken up with Him, that He may enlighten you to His will for your life. For all sin is displeasing to our Father in Heaven.

Sexual immorality is the engagement in sexual acts outside of a husband and wife enjoying each other. There are many scriptures that warn us against being sexually immoral, such as 1 Corinthians 6:9, Ephesians 5:5, and Galatians 5:19 to name a few from a long list. There are also many forms of sexual immorality that we must be aware of according to the Bible, such as fornication, homosexuality, adultery, and prostitution. Our spiritual mirror also warns us against lustful desires and sensuality—which would add to this list—watching pornography, and masturbation. Even then the list would be incomplete. Throughout God's Word, we are encouraged to live pure and holy lives and to have self-control. Sexual immorality is advertised all around us every day. TV shows, commercials, books, magazines, and even people out in public fail to give us a break from sexual implications and indecencies. Young man, without self-control we are sure to buy into what Satan is selling sooner rather than later.

With that being said, let's talk about sex and the dangers of fornication. Let's talk about why you should ignore the world's demand to indulge in sexual pleasures and instead run away from it. I know—not the popular choice, but when I tell you it is necessary, believe me, it's necessary. Run away!

I was in the fifth grade the first time I remember being asked if I was a virgin or not. I was, and I answered truthfully because I didn't think anyone was having sex yet at my age. Heck, I still thought French kissing was nasty and was still afraid to touch girls on the behind like some of my male classmates were doing. That same school year, I was approached by a girl in my class, and she said that she wanted to kiss me after school. A couple of my friends were there when she asked me, so rather than seem afraid, I said, "Cool...let's do it." My friends cheered with excitement as if they couldn't wait to see it happen. One of them threw his arm around my shoulder as we walked away, as if he was proud of the step I was about to take.

What my friends didn't know, though, is that I was nervous. I didn't think it was right to be kissing girls at that age, and I didn't even know how to kiss. I had also already accepted Christ by this time, so I didn't think it fell in line with being saved either. Throughout the rest of the school day, I thought of ways to get out of kissing her after school. Unable to think of a good excuse, I decided to just act as if I had forgotten. The bell rang for dismissal, I headed toward the classroom exit, and there she was, waiting for me. She looked at me and asked, "Are you ready?" but when I noticed my friends were not by the door, I said, "Nah," and walked away. Of course, my friends found out what I did, and they teased me. Innocently enough, I defended myself by explaining to them how nasty kissing was. The kiss that didn't happen was soon forgotten, and it was back to fifth grade as usual for me.

That was the first time that I ran away from a sexual encounter, however innocent it may seem. The problem is that I would indulge in that first kiss about a year later, sparking a desire for sexual intimacy that would prove to be difficult to contain. I get it, young brother; it was just a kiss, you say. However, that kiss led to my desire for another one and another one, then another one with some touching, and soon the kissing and touching wasn't enough. I wanted to go all the way and would push the limits with every kiss until it happened. Some of my friends were experiencing the same thing. We were tiptoeing around sex, and although we wanted to experience it, we just couldn't seem to make it happen. Without placing any bets or saying anything verbally, it was understood that the race to lose our virginity was on.

Sadly, the race ended for me by the age of thirteen. I had crossed the finish line, and I was no longer a virgin. I couldn't wait to tell my friends! I wasn't doing a good job of putting Christ first at age thirteen, so I didn't feel guilty. I knew I had done something wrong, but I was happy about losing my virginity. Young man, if you find yourself happy after sinning against God, you are not in the right relationship with Christ. I was not in the right relationship with Christ. My desire to please my flesh meant more to me than pleasing God at that time. Is there anything in your life that you desire more than pleasing God? Maybe not, or maybe you've never seriously asked yourself that question. However, if you ever feel like a winner after yielding to sin, you might have your answer. I felt like I had won because the cloud of being a virgin was no longer over me. The reality was that I had just suffered arguably the biggest loss of my life.

One obvious thing that I lost was my virginity. When I lost my virginity, I also ruined the opportunity to please God by holding on to something that He wanted me to save for my wife. My virginity was sacred, and once I gave it away, I could not get it back. God created sex for our pleasure; however, by His design, this pleasure was created for a man and his wife to enjoy together. Otherwise, we fornicate, which is a form of sexual immorality. We find evidence of this in our spiritual mirror.

Consider this scripture, young man: "Let marriage be had in honor among all, and let the bed be undefiled: for fornicators and adulterers God will judge" (Hebrews 13:4, ASV). This scripture teaches us that sex within a marriage is sexual purity. However, sex outside of marriage, be it before marriage or with someone other than your wife, is sexually immoral and comes with judgment from God. I urge you, brothers, to present your body as a living sacrifice, holy and pleasing to God (Romans 12:1). If you still have your virginity, hold on to it. Your bodies are members of Christ Himself and therefore should not be united with anyone in a sinful manner (1 Corinthians 6:15–17). If you no longer have it, repent and turn away from sexual immorality. For the body is not meant for sexual immorality but for the Lord, and the Lord for the body (1 Corinthians 6:13).

Having sex for the first time also introduced me to struggles that I never saw coming. I couldn't wait to do it again. My conversations with females changed, and I was constantly searching for that climactic feeling again. That is what sexual immorality does, my young brother. When we indulge, it causes us to desire that sinful experience again and again. I guess it's fair to say that before having sex, I didn't know what I was missing. I didn't. My desire to have sex then was rooted in peer influence and, of course, natural hormones. However, after experiencing sex, the foundation of my desire to do it again was the feeling I experienced from satisfying my flesh (climaxing). Desiring that feeling again drove my sexual desires and opened the door for me to consider other forms of sexual immorality, such as pornography and masturbation.

Get this, young man: although I may have indulged in a few inappropriate photos of women in a magazine, I had never watched pornography or practiced masturbation prior to having sex. As I reflect, there may have been a reason for that. You see, before having a climactic sexual experience, I didn't even know what feeling I was trying to bring about, nor did I know how to get myself there. I didn't know what I was missing, and it was best for me not to know. However, once I knew, I practiced sexually immoral acts to feel it again.

Once fornication becomes a habit, it's easy to start passing it off as just a common "necessity" for men. It is possible to stop viewing it as the sin that it is. Bad sexual habits can even cause you to start justifying your sinful actions. For example, masturbation becomes the alternative for sex, but you feel good about it because at least you are not *really* having sex. Or watching pornography becomes okay because you're not masturbating or having sex. We must remember that it is all sin, and any sinful alternative still feeds the habit. I never considered myself to have an addiction to anything. However, my continued practice of sexual immorality for several years after losing my virginity comes close. After I rededicated my life to Christ during my senior year of high school, this struggle is one that would rear its ugly head for many years later. I use the term *struggle* instead of *practice* because I was no longer a slave to the sin of sexual immorality.

My inner being wanted to please God; however, my inner being was at war with the desires of my flesh (Romans 7:21–25). Just because we struggle, young man, does not mean we continue to yield to temptation. No! God is faithful; He will not let you be tempted beyond what you can bear. But when you are tempted, He will also provide a way out (1 Corinthians 10:12–13). It is up to us, young man, to use the way out that God has provided. It's up to us to run away. Let's look at a biblical example found in the book of Genesis 39:1–12 (MSG) and see what we can learn from Joseph:

After Joseph had been taken to Egypt by the Ishmaelites, Potiphar an Egyptian, one of Pharaoh's officials and the manager of his household, bought him from them.

As it turned out, God was with Joseph and things went very well with him. He ended up living in the home of his Egyptian master. His master recognized that God was with him, saw that God was working for good in everything he did. He became very fond of Joseph and made him his personal aide. He put him in charge of all his personal affairs, turning everything over to him. From that moment on, God blessed the home of the Egyptian—all because of Joseph. The blessing of God spread over everything he owned, at home and in the fields, and all Potiphar had to concern himself with was eating three meals a day.

Joseph was a strikingly handsome man. As time went on, his master's wife became infatuated with Joseph and one day said, "Sleep with me."

He wouldn't do it. He said to his master's wife, "Look, with me here, my master doesn't give a second thought to anything that goes on here—he's put me in charge of everything he owns. He treats me as an equal. The only thing he hasn't turned over to me is you. You're his wife, after all! How could I violate his trust and sin against God?"

She pestered him day after day after day, but he stood his ground. He refused to go to bed with her.

On one of these days he came to the house to do his work and none of the household servants happened to be there. She grabbed him by his cloak, saying, "Sleep with me!" He left his coat in her hand and ran out of the house.

Young brother, there are many lessons that we could pull from this passage of scripture, but I want you to focus on the fact that Joseph cared more about walking upright and pleasing God than he did his flesh. Sure, he had an opportunity to be sexually immoral, and he was tempted by another man's wife, but Joseph did not take the bait. Instead he ran away! Even though he had free will, he ran away. Joseph did not flirt with the idea of sleeping with his master's wife. He didn't kiss and touch or see how far it would go before trying to stop. He ran away!

Young man, we all have free will. However, just because something is permissible doesn't mean that it is beneficial or spiritually appropriate (1 Corinthians 6:12). We also have very clear instructions from our Father in Heaven. He has even given us a clear mirror to look into in order to clothe ourselves with righteousness. The world has taught young men for far too long that a long list of sexually immoral encounters with females should be worn as a badge of honor. But no longer can we fall for that. Do not be fooled by the mirrors of the world, for the wicked hide within them.

Do you not know that the wicked will not inherit the kingdom of God? Do not be deceived: neither the sexually immoral, nor idolaters, nor adulterers, nor men who submit to homosexual acts, nor thieves, nor the greedy, nor drunkards, nor verbal abusers, nor swindlers, will inherit the kingdom of God. And that is what some of you were. But you were washed, you were sanctified, you were justified, in the name of the Lord Jesus Christ and by the Spirit of our God. (1 Corinthians 6:9–11, BSB)

We must make a decision to live for Christ, young man, and in order to do that, we must honor God with our bodies.

Flee from sexual immorality. All other sins a person commits are outside the body, but whoever sins sexually, sins against their own body. Do you not know that your bodies are temples of the Holy Spirit, who is in you, whom you have received from God? You are not your own; you were bought at a price. Therefore honor God with your bodies. (1 Corinthians 6:18– 20, NIV)

Chapter 9

EVEN IN YOUR DREAMS

Dreams seem to be a very common occurrence for human beings. When we lie down to sleep, there is really no telling how our mind will wander or what pictures, events, and even memories will surface and be presented as a motion picture—often starring you. Some dreams are pleasant. Those that highlight the best memories of our lives, those that make hopes and future goals feel like present realities, and those that feed our sexual desires are often the ones we don't mind having. They even contribute to us waking up in a good mood from time to time. Then there are dreams that we just wish we didn't have—you know, the dreams that wake you up in the middle of the night and make your heart beat a little faster. Yeah, those dreams. And lastly, we sometimes have dreams that just don't make any sense to us, so we easily cast them away and place them in the weird dream box.

But what is a dream, really? Why do we have them? According to a WebMD article titled "Dreams" by Dr. Carol DerSarkissian, dreams are "stories and images that our mind creates while we sleep." There are many theories about why we dream, but no one knows for sure. Sigmund Freud, a famous psychologist, believed that dreams are a window into our subconscious and that they reveal a person's unconscious desires, thoughts, and motivations. Others say that our dreams reflect our deepest desires, fears, and concerns. Regardless of what our dreams reflect, studies show that our most vivid dreams happen at a time during our sleep when our brain is most active. If our brains are active during our sleep, does that mean that we have some control in our dreams or that we can make choices? I want you to ponder that question as I share with you my most vivid life-changing experience.

It was late. I was tired, so I said my prayers and climbed in the bed to get some much-needed rest. Little did I know, though, I was about to have an experience with God that would forever change my perspective. That experience started as a dream.

In this dream I kept waking up in different rooms, and each room that I woke up in had a bed in it. After waking up in several different rooms, the last room that I woke up in was a bit larger, and the bed that I was lying in was circular shaped. When I woke up in that particular bed, I remember thinking that I needed to get up and leave. So I got out of the bed and left the room. As soon as I opened the door, I stepped into a poorly lit hallway with red lighting. As I looked to my left and then to my right, I could tell I was in some sort of hotel. However, as I looked left and right, I also noticed that the hallway was so long on both sides that I could not see the end of it. I did manage to see what appeared to be an exit sign, so I decided to start walking in that direction.

As soon as I started walking toward that exit, I noticed a young lady approaching. Although I couldn't make out any facial features, I remember her being short, about four and a half feet tall at best, and extremely skinny with black hair that stopped a little lower than her shoulders. As she approached, she intercepted my path and asked me where I was going in a really sweet voice. I told her I had to leave. I remember feeling like I had been gone way too long and had no sense of the time or date since I had been asleep in so many different places. She told me I shouldn't leave, and she stepped around me and slipped her left arm inside my right arm. "You're tired," she said. "You should get some more rest." Since I really was tired in the dream, I did not resist her. Instead I said, "You're right," and allowed her to escort me back to the room.

As we entered the room, there was the white circular-shaped bed. It was really thin, almost like a tabletop, and it was spinning very slowly. She led me to the bed and helped me get in it, and I lay down. She then climbed in the bed, crawled across me, and lay down next to me on my left side. After lying there for a while, I felt the sudden urge to leave again. I said, "Okay, I really need to go. I have to get home." Before I could even sit up, she crawled across my body and lay down on my right side, this time looping her left arm in my right arm and gently caressing my chest with her right hand. When she did this, I knew that things were turning sexual, but for some reason, it just didn't feel right. Her rubbing on my chest felt way too good—better than normal. It felt so good that I said, "No, I need to go," and attempted to get up and leave. But she pulled me close and started to kiss me on my neck. When she kissed me on my neck, it felt even better than the feeling I felt when she caressed my chest. Her kissing me on my neck felt so good that it seemed supernatural, even though it was in my dream. It felt so good that I yelled "stop!" in my dream and woke up.

Now before I go any further, let me be very clear about one thing. When I say I woke up, what I mean is that I literally woke up to reality. I opened my eyes to a pitch-black room but was able to recognize that I was in my room, in the basement of my sister's house, which is where I was living at the time. I was fully awake and fully aware. Although I was no longer in my dream, I still felt that supernatural feeling that I felt while I was dreaming. Not only that but I also still felt the young lady clinging to my right arm and kissing me on my neck, giving me a pleasurable feeling that I had never felt before. Yes, I had indulged in sexual behavior with women many times before, and the desires of my flesh were physically fulfilled. But this feeling was different—very different.

Gripped with disbelief, I yelled out in a loud voice, "In the name of Jesus, make her stop!" I felt her loosen her hold on me, but she then pulled me closer, held me tighter, and started to kiss my neck again. This time the feeling was even better, paralyzing me from the waist up. I then yelled out even louder, saying, "In the name of Jesus, make her stop!" She loosened her grip on me again but pulled me even closer and held me even tighter. She began to kiss me on my neck a third time. This time the feeling was so good that it paralyzed my entire body. I felt a warm sensation flow down through my legs all the way to the tips of my toes. Knowing this was something that I could not fight but determined not to yield to it, I cried out in the loudest voice I could, saying, "In the name of Jesus, make her stop!" This time she jumped off me and ran, vanishing through the wall.

I regained the use of my limbs, and that warm sensation that seemed to be running through my veins was gone. The darkness in the room was not as dark anymore, and I sat up, halfway slumped over in my bed. I held my ribs on my right side because I could still feel where some part of her body was digging into my side from clinging to me so tightly. I was breathing heavily, seemingly trying to regain the breath that she took out of me. As I sat there, slumped over and breathing closer to normal, I heard the Lord Jesus speak to me in a small voice. He said these words to me: "Even in your unconscious state of mind, your mind must be stayed on Me."

After hearing this I felt a sense of comfort and covering. I knew that I had wrestled with a demon attached to my sexual desires and my huge struggle with sexual immorality, but I found comfort in knowing that Jesus was there with me. His name alone was enough to deliver me from the hand of the enemy. Knowing this, I lay back down and went back to sleep.

I wish I could say that was the last time that I was tempted sexually in a dream, but it wasn't. While I have not had another experience as serious as the one I described above, I continue to have dreams that tempt me to be sexually immoral. Now most people, and some of you who are reading this, would probably say, "It's just a dream, so what's the big deal? People do things in dreams all the time, but it's not like you're doing it in real life." My response, though, is this. I hear you loud and clear. But maybe you, and most others, have never heard it explained like this before.

We have been conditioned to believe that what we do in dreams doesn't matter and that we have free rein to do what we want to do in dreams. And I get it because nobody has ever said anything different—until now. The truth is we make choices in our dreams just like we do when we are wide awake. Do we always make the right choices? No, but we do have control, and I am a living witness to that. Even in our dreams, we make decisions to do certain things, but the irony is that oftentimes we do not decide to say no to the things we shouldn't do.

I'll use myself as an example. I never said no to sexual pleasures in a dream until that night in 2011. I, too, was of the anything-goes mindset when it came to dreams. However, after that experience, I—with God's help, of course—have been able to resist Satan, even in my dreams. I don't get it right every time, but the important thing is that I have a consciousness of what is happening, and since my brain is still working, I remember Jesus, and then I can overcome. I am not perfect when I'm awake, but the same is true, with Jesus I can overcome.

I don't want to lose you, but understand this: if the enemy can attack us when we are awake, we are not off-limits when we're asleep. That is why we pray before going to bed. We don't pray out of habit before going to bed. We pray before bed because we need God to keep us and keep our minds so that the enemy doesn't take advantage of us while we sleep. If I fail God in my dreams, I repent when I wake up because I want to please Him, and I remember what He told me: "Even in your unconscious state of mind, your mind must be stayed on Me." Therefore, I know that we can overcome, but we have to want to. We must desire to please God so much that we are willing to try a new thing. We make a decision to fight and protect ourselves in dreams. We make decisions to run away when we are afraid in our dreams. We make decisions to satisfy our flesh through sexual immorality in our dreams.

So why not try something different? Why not make a decision to please God in a dream? Why not remember that you are saved and that the enemy has already been defeated in your dream? You should give it a try out of your desire to please God, and if you ever feel stuck, call on the name of Jesus. I'll also push you to do this: call His name and believe that He will fight for you. You can change the narrative, young man, even in your dreams.

It is not the will of God that we be overcome by sin. I believe that God has given us victory in every aspect of our lives in which we put Him at the center. Listen, if we are going to even attempt to resist Satan and cause him to flee, be it while awake or asleep, we must draw closer to Christ. We must read our Bible, reflect, repent, pray, and remember. We must whisper a prayer at random times during the day in order to keep Christ at the forefront of our hearts and minds. *We must spend time with God.* That means that we have to not only pray but also spend time reading His Word and meditating on it.

It is His will to keep you and rescue you. He desires to save the day for you. You need only to surrender your all to Him, even in your dreams.

Chapter 10

SEE IT, AND HIT IT

There is no better place to be than in the will of God. There is no better path to walk than the straight and narrow, which leads to eternal life with Christ. This I am sure of. Satan knows this too, and he is determined to not only knock you off but also keep you off track. Don't let that happen. I'm telling you now: *Satan will throw very familiar temptations at you to cause your fall.* He will also present you with some of your biggest pet peeves and things that he thinks will cause you to stumble. You must remember whom you represent: you represent Christ.

My elder brother says that when I was young, I was pretty much a natural when it came to baseball. He claims that with his help, I was hitting hoops, or underhand pitches, at age three. While I don't remember much about what happened when I was three years old, I take his word for it. I also learned from others in my family that during my T-ball games I would often hit the ball, then run the wrong way. They said that whenever I would do this, my dad would have to come onto the field and turn me around in order to put me back on the proper path. I'm not really sure why I did this, but I can think of a couple of reasons why it would have made sense to me.

For starters, I'd argue that it would have been a lot easier to score if I started from third base. Skipping first and second would have been game-changing. All I would have to do then was make it to home plate. Also, depending on where the ball went when I hit it, running to third base, instead of first base, may have lessened my chances of getting out. I may have been a natural, but I clearly didn't have the best understanding of the rules. It doesn't matter how good you are at something or how much of a natural you are; if you don't know the rules of what you're playing or doing, you're not going to be successful. Actually, you're going to suck at it. The rules of a game or a sport make it unique and make it what it is. Rules determine how something is done or how something is played. Try playing baseball with basketball rules. Impossible! Soccer with baseball rules. Can't do it!

Yes, some games and sports have similar rules, but there is always something that makes them different.

Not only are there rules of a game but there are also fundamental rules that one must remember in order to develop, become proficient, and master certain skills needed to play the game and at more advanced levels. Arguably the most complicated yet majorly important skill needed to be successful at baseball is hitting. There is much to remember when learning to hit and trying to become good at it. Spread your feet, bend your knees, don't hold the bat too tight, relax, keep your front elbow down, close the space between your hands, keep your eyes on the ball, swing all the way through, keep your weight back, rotate your hips—and the list goes on.

As a beginner or an experienced hitter, though, there is one simple rule that must be followed, and that applies on every level of play: see the ball, hit the ball. Every baseball coach whom I have ever had has spoken this rule in some form or fashion. Some would say, "You can't hit what you can't see," and others would simply say, "See it, and hit it." It makes perfect sense. You have to see the ball to hit the ball, especially if you want to hit it consistently. If you weren't focused and watching the ball, you probably weren't going to hit it, and eventually, you would strike out. You must keep your eye on the ball and make a decision on how you are going to handle the pitch. Will you let it go because swinging at it is not worth the effort? Will you watch it enter your zone, and allow it to cause a strike against you? Or will you swing, knock the pitch out of the park, and discourage the pitcher from throwing that pitch to you again, which limits his arsenal against you? You would probably choose the latter.

Now before I go any further, I want to be clear that I am not suggesting that you treat life like a game, young man. I do, however, want you to stay with me while I make a connection between our lives and the game of baseball. Each one of us may be at a different level in our faith walk. Some of us are in T-ball or just beginning our Christian journey. Some have been following Christ for a few years. Others have been facing the devil's pitches for many years. Wherever we are in our faith, we all have to keep the rules in our hearts and minds in order to be better Christians. Sure, trying to be a good Christian can feel a lot like trying to hit the fastest curveballs sometimes. So many rules, right? The twentieth chapter of Exodus gives us ten rules, better known as the Ten Commandments:

1. Have no other gods before our God.
2. Do not worship any idol gods. Worship our God only.
3. Do not use God's name in curses or playful manners.
4. Keep the Sabbath Day holy.
5. Honor your father and your mother.
6. Do not murder.
7. Do not commit adultery.
8. Do not steal.
9. Always tell the truth.
10. Do not lust for what your neighbor has; don't be jealous.

While trying to remember ten rules in our daily lives can seem overwhelming, Jesus gave us an easy way to be conscious of all ten as well as a way to remember what being a Christian is all about. He summed it up with two commands that apply to every level of our Christian journey:

1. Love the Lord your God with all your heart and with all your soul and with all your mind (Matthew 22:37).
2. Love your neighbor as yourself (Matthew 22:39).

Everything hangs on these two commandments (Matthew 22:40). If we remember to love God and love people on a daily basis, we will be better prepared when facing Satan's arsenal of pitches. If we focus and lock in on these two commands, we will be able to see Satan's pitch as soon as it leaves his hand. This is super important because Satan has been watching you and already knows your weakness. He knows if you struggle with sex, drugs, language, lying, stealing, or whatever your struggle may be. So then his pitch is to lure you into situations in which he thinks you will not please God. He wants you to respond to that text, the one where the girl says she is home alone and wants you to come over. He wants you to go to the party where everybody is drinking and smoking, especially if that used to be your thing. He wants you to get irritated and frustrated so that you will curse someone out. He wants you to be jealous of others so that you will lie and steal. He is going to throw that pitch, and until you see it and hit it out of your mind or until you are able to say, "I love God and people too much to fall for that again," he is going to keep throwing it. Proving that you can be successful in your areas of weakness will destabilize his expectations of you in the future. Don't continue to yield to the same temptations and commit the same sins, causing you to strike out. Knock it out of the park! Make Satan choose another pitch to throw. Yes, he will throw other pitches, but with Christ as your coach, you will learn to hit those too.

If you are new to this Christian journey or if you have been on the team for a good while but haven't been practicing (reading God's Word, reflecting, praying, and remembering), you might not find success as much as you would like. Even if you are an experienced Christian, you may struggle with the rules and run the wrong way sometimes. The beautiful thing is even if you do, God is always there to turn you around and set you on the proper path. See it, and hit it, young man. Then run—run toward Christ.

Acknowledgments

To God the Father, God the Son, and God the Holy Spirit, I am forever indebted to You. I thank You for Your grace and mercy, for loving me—even when I didn't love myself—and for continuing to love me, even now, with all of my imperfections. You are my hero. You rescued me from the hand of the enemy. Your grace is sufficient, and Your power is made perfect in my weakness. I could never repay You for what You have done for me, but here I am; I'm ready to go, and I'm going public with my love for You.

To my beautiful wife, thank you for being patient with me and understanding that God is not finished with me yet. Thank you for continuing to love me when I am not my best self. Thank you for your encouragement along the way. Thank you for giving me the space needed to write this book and for every prayer you lifted up for God's will in my life. You, me, and God—though we're three—are a perfect pair, and we'll face each day forever, come what may. I love you, DeMoya.

To my son, thank you for giving me the breaks I needed from playing video games with you so that I could write this book. Thank you for understanding that Daddy loves you, even when I can't play with you in the moment. Thank you for praying for me. You are the best son I could ever ask for. I want to be like you when I grow up. Don't forget my teaching, son. Trust God, be you, influence the world around you, and strive to be great each day. Daddy loves you.

To my parents, the late Reverend Jonathan Brown Jr. and Mrs. Mary Brown, thank you for introducing me to Christ. Thank you for teaching me the importance of walking in His ways. You trained me up in the way that I should go, and here I am, still trusting in the Lord. Thank you for showing me what commitment to God and commitment to marriage looks like. Dad, I will never forget your teaching, your example. Rest in peace. Mom, your strength and faith in God will always be something that I admire. I'm grateful to have known both of you.

To my siblings, Dietrich Brown (Tonja), Leslie Alexander (Reginald), and Melva Brown, thank you for being my biggest fans and for all the times you surrendered your ears to my thoughts. Your friendship is irreplaceable, and I love y'all tremendously. Melva, your advice, knowledge of God's Word, and perspective were instrumental to me during the process of writing this book. Thank you for pushing me, challenging me, and encouraging me to write with purpose. To my mother- and father-in-law, Mama Watson and Papa Watson, thank you for your prayers and guidance. I appreciate and love you both. To my entire in-law family, thank you for welcoming me and loving me as I am. To my fraternity brother and friend Pastor Johnnie Miller Jr., thank you for your insight and the attention you gave to this book. To my remaining family and friends, thank you for being the best village I could ask for.

Finally, to my church families, past and present, thank you. Growing up as a pastor's kid, I was taught the importance of not only attending church but also being an active member of a church. To my current pastor, Reverend Dr. Howard-John Wesley, and church family at Alfred Street Baptist Church (Alexandria, Virginia), thank you for inspiring me to be a better Christian and to strengthen my walk with Christ. To the various United Methodist churches where my dad pastored while I was growing up, thank you. To my uncle, Pastor Weston Burgess Jr. and the Mount Seal Missionary Baptist Church family (Lake City, South Carolina), thank you for filling my younger years with valuable teachings that I carry with me, even now.

About the Author

Decius Brown attended Claflin University where he played baseball and majored in physical education. He holds a master's degree in athletic administration from Ohio University. He is currently a dean of students at a Washington, DC based high school and has been working in the field of education for seventeen years. When not writing, he enjoys mentoring and helping youth harness their potential. He believes that leading others to Christ and helping others strengthen their relationship with God is his life's purpose. Decius is the Founder and CEO of Run Toward Christ, an organization created to help young Christians thrive. He currently resides in Maryland with his wife and son.

You can follow Decius and request him for speaking engagements at the following links:

www.runtowardchrist.com

Instagram: @deciusobrown

Facebook.com/deciusbrown

Twitter: @deciusobrown